The Maya
In the Past and Present

John Perritano

PICTURE CREDITS

Cover (foreground) © Frans Lemmens/zefa/Corbis; cover (background) © Angelo Cavalli/Getty Images; title page, page 36 © Scala/Art Resource, NY; pages 2-3, 16-23 (borders) © Dave Bartruff/Getty Images; pages 4-5, 25 (top left), 34-a map illustrations by Paul Mirocha; pages 6-7 © Kenneth Garrett/National Geographic Image Collection; page 8 © Kimbell Art Museum/Corbis; pages 8-13 (backgrounds) © Panoramic Images/Getty Images; pages 9, 25 (bottom left), 34-b Roy H. Andersen/National Geographic Society; pages 10, 31 (bottom left) illustrations by Alan Witschonke; pages 11 (top left), 11 (top right), 11 (bottom left), 31 (center left) © Corbis; pages 11 (bottom right), 25 (top right), 34-f © Brand X Pictures/Getty Images; pages 12, 30 (bottom), 31 (bottom right), 34-c © H. Tom Hall/National Geographic Society; pages 13 (bottom left), 35-e © Stephen Frink/Corbis; page 13 (bottom center) © Bob Krist/Corbis; pages 13 (bottom right), 34-e © Charles & Josette Lenars/Corbis; page 13 (top) © Kevin Schafer/Getty Images; page 14 (inset), 20, 22, 25 (bottom right), 28, 31 (center right), 35-c © Danny Lehman/Corbis; pages 15, 34-d © Vanni Archive/Corbis; pages 16-17 © Gianni Vecchiato; pages 18, 31 (top right) © Owen Franken/Corbis; pages 19, 35-a © Tibor Bognár/Corbis; page 21 © David Alan Harvey/Magnum Photos; pages 23, 35-d © Thomas Hoepker/Magnum Photos; page 26 (top) © Neil Beer/Getty Images; page 26 (bottom) © 2005 Banco de México Diego Rivera & Frida Kahlo Museums Trust/Underwood Photo Archives/SuperStock; page 27 © Artephot/Corbis; page 29 © Michael Holford; page 30 (top) © Erich Lessing/Art Resource, NY; pages 31 (top left), 35-b © Nik Wheeler/Corbis; page 32 © Werner Forman/Corbis; page 33 (left) *Mexico* by Kevin Supples, © 2002 National Geographic Society, photo © Kenneth Garrett; page 33 (center) *Peru* by Helen Byers, © 2004 National Geographic Society, photo © Jeremy Horner/Corbis; page 33 (right) *The First Civilizations*, © 2005 National Geographic Society, photo © Bill Elzey/National Geographic Image Collection.

Produced through the worldwide resources of the National Geographic Society, John M. Fahey, Jr., President and Chief Executive Officer; Gilbert M. Grosvenor, Chairman of the Board; Nina D. Hoffman, Executive Vice President and President, Books and Education Publishing Group.

PREPARED BY NATIONAL GEOGRAPHIC SCHOOL PUBLISHING

Ericka Markman, Senior Vice President and President, Children's Books and Education Publishing Group; Steve Mico, Senior Vice President, Editorial Director, Publisher; Francis Downey, Executive Editor; Richard Easby, Editorial Manager; Anne Stone, Lori Dibble Collins, Editors; Bea Jackson, Director of Layout and Design; Jim Hiscott, Design Manager; Cynthia Olson, Art Director; Margaret Sidlosky, Illustrations Director; Matt Wascavage, Manager of Publishing Services; Sean Philpotts, Production Manager; Ted Tucker, Production Specialist.

MANUFACTURING AND QUALITY CONTROL

Christopher A. Liedel, Chief Financial Officer; Phillip L. Schlosser, Director; Clifton M. Brown III, Manager

CONSULTANT AND REVIEWER

Claudia Bautista Nicholas

BOOK DESIGN/PHOTO RESEARCH

Steve Curtis Design, Inc.

◄ The Maya of today are known for their beautiful weaving.

Contents

Copyright © 2006 National Geographic Society.
All Rights Reserved. Reproduction of the whole or any part of the
contents without written permission from the publisher is prohibited.
National Geographic, National Geographic School Publishing,
National Geographic Reading Expeditions, and the Yellow Border
are registered trademarks of the National Geographic Society.

Published by the National Geographic Society
1145 17th Street N.W.
Washington, D.C. 20036-4688

ISBN-13: 978-0-7922-5463-8
ISBN-10: 0-7922-5463-5

2014
     4 5 6 7 8 9 10 11 12 13 14 15

Printed in Canada.

Mexico and Central America

Look at the map. It shows Mexico and Central America. In **ancient** times, this area was home to many different groups of people. One of those groups was the Maya. The Maya lived about 1,400 years ago.

Mexico and Central America have many rain forests. These forests are warm and wet. Every bit of space is covered by trees and vines. The ancient Maya lived deep in the rain forests. Their homes were hidden among the trees.

....

ancient — very old or from very long ago

North America

Mexico and Central America

South America

4

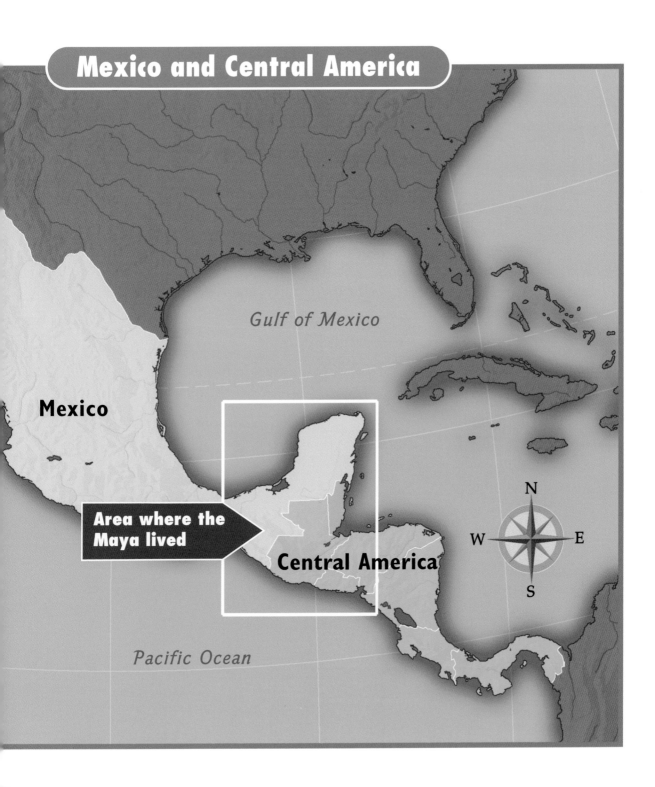

Mexico and Central America

Gulf of Mexico

Mexico

Area where the Maya lived

Central America

Pacific Ocean

N
W   E
S

THE WORLD O MA

Big Idea
The Maya created one of the earliest great civilizations.

Set Purpose
Read to learn how the ancient Maya lived.

The Maya were among the first people to live in the Americas. They built large cities in the rain forest. The Maya worked, lived, and played in these cities. The Maya also built **pyramids** as part of their religion. Today, many people visit the **ruins** of these ancient wonders.

pyramid — a building with four sides that come together to form a point
ruins — the remains of old buildings

Questions You Will Explore

What are the Maya famous for?

How did the ancient Maya live?

F THE

YA

▲ Ancient Maya ruins rise
from the rain forest.

Chiefs and City-States

The Maya built big cities called **city-states**.
Each city-state had its own laws and rules.
Each had its own ruler, or **chief**. The chief was
usually a man. He ruled until he died. Then his
son became the chief. City-states were often
built around a pyramid. They also had temples
and monuments. Many people lived in or near
a city-state.

city-state – a settlement or city with its own government
chief – the leader of a tribe of people

▶ **This is an ancient
statue of a Maya chief.**

Gods and Religion

The Maya believed in many gods and goddesses. All the Maya gods came from nature. For example, the Maya had a sun god. They thought the sun god was the father of the Maya people.

Maya chiefs spoke to the gods. They asked for rain and sun. Priests were nearly as powerful as chiefs. Priests held weddings and other **ceremonies**.

....

ceremony — a formal act done on a special occasion

▼ **Ceremonies were sometimes held at pyramids.**

Maya Homes

Some people lived in or near a city-state. But many others lived in small villages. They built homes out of mud, vines, wood, and stone. These homes had only one or two rooms. They had roofs of heavy grass. Women cooked outside over open fires.

▼ This drawing shows what a Maya village might have looked like long ago.

Farming the Land

Most Maya were skilled farmers. They grew tomatoes, chili peppers, and sweet potatoes. Their most important crop was **maize,** or corn. The Maya thought corn was a gift from the gods.

The Maya ground corn into cornmeal to make tortillas. Tortillas are a traditional thin bread. The Maya also raised bees for honey. The Maya ate meat only at special times of the year.

....
maize – corn

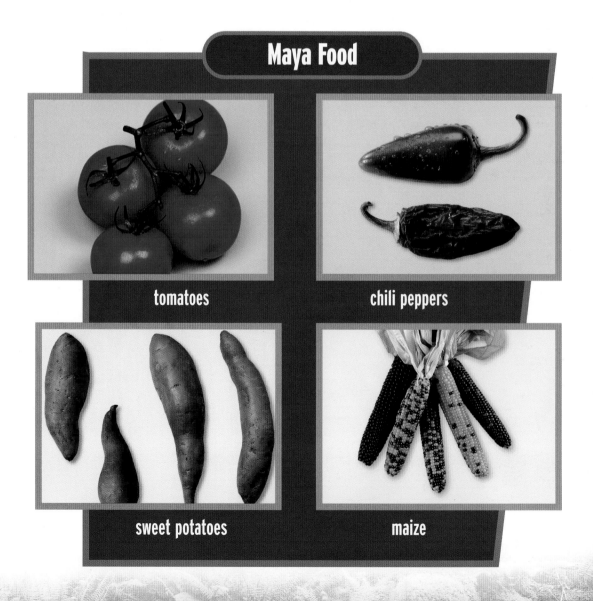

Maya Food

tomatoes

chili peppers

sweet potatoes

maize

Maya Clothing

Most ancient Maya wore plain clothing.
Women wore skirts or loose dresses. Men
wrapped simple coverings around their waists.
But chiefs had fancy clothes. They wore
colorful headdresses with feathers. They wore
necklaces and bracelets, too. These were often
carved from a green stone called **jade.**

....
jade – a green stone

▼ Chiefs wore colorful clothing and jewels.

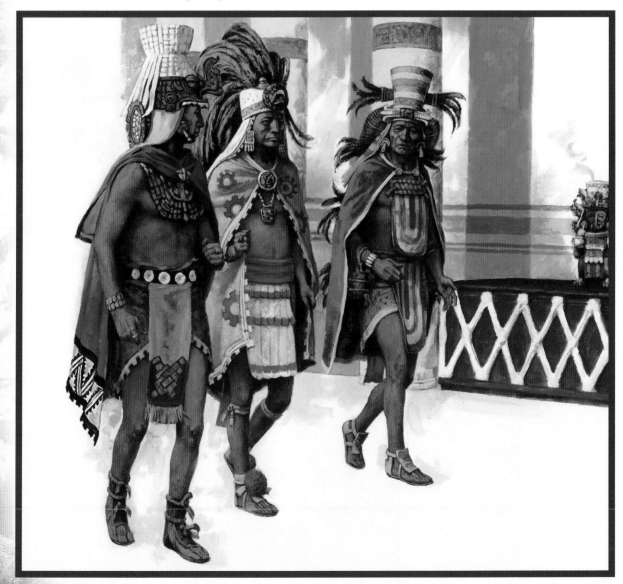

Trading for Goods

The Maya traded with one another for many different goods. Maya living by the ocean gathered seashells. Traders took these shells to the jungle. They traded with Maya living there for jade.

The Maya traded other **valuable** things. They traded bird feathers. They also traded salt. The Maya needed salt to preserve, or dry, their food. Dried food can be stored for a long time.

....
valuable – worth a lot

▼ Feathers from the quetzal bird were very valuable.

Trading Goods

seashells

salt

jade

Maya Art

The Maya had many jobs. Most were farmers.
Some were soldiers, traders, or **merchants.**
Others were artists and craftsmen. Potters
made pots, and weavers wove cloth. Painters
painted murals. Sculptors carved designs in
wood and stone.

....
merchant — a person who sells things

▲ **This is a wood carving
of the Maya sun god.**

A Rich Culture

The ancient Maya had a rich culture.
They built big cities. They created a
government. They painted beautiful
pictures and learned how to write.
The Maya invented a calendar much like
ours. They also were among the first to map
the stars. The Maya did all this more than a
thousand years ago!

Stop and Think!

What was life like for
the ancient Maya?

▼ **These are ruins of an
ancient Maya palace.**

Recap
Explain how the
ancient Maya lived
and worked.

Set Purpose
Look at what Maya
life is like today.

Maya Life Today

There are four million Maya living in Mexico and Central America today. The Maya speak some of the same languages as long ago. They eat some of the same foods. They worship some of the same gods. The Maya carry on traditions from ancient times.

Homes Today

Many Maya choose to live in small villages like the Maya of long ago. They build the same kinds of homes. These homes are small but well made. They are cool in the summer heat. Yet the rooms are easy to heat when the weather is cold. Roofs are steep and made of grasses or palm leaves. They keep out heavy rains.

▲ Maya homes are built with mud, stone, grass, and wood.

Family Life

Maya women are in charge of cooking. Most homes do not have a stove. So women usually cook outside as they did long ago. They shop for food at local markets. A family might also own a few goats and chickens. These provide milk and eggs. Families get water from nearby wells.

▼ **Women shop for vegetables at a local market.**

Sewing and Weaving

The Maya live in a warm place. To keep cool, they wear light cotton clothes. Many of these clothes are homemade. The Maya weave their own cloth, just as in ancient times. Women sew shirts and dresses. Men braid rope and twine.

▼ A Maya woman weaves cloth for a hammock.

Farming Today

Many Maya still grow their own food. Farmers plant the same types of crops as long ago. Men tend the fields. Women grind the corn to make tortillas. People share the work that must be done.

▲ **Men plant crops using traditional tools.**

Religion Today

Religion is as important today as in the past.
Some people follow religions such as Christianity.
Other people believe in the traditional gods. The
Maya still celebrate many festivals and holidays.
They like to perform ancient songs and dances.
On special days, some people still wear bright
costumes and masks.

▲ Maya gather in front
of a church.

Telling Stories of the Past

Today, many **tourists** travel to see the ruins of ancient Maya cities. The ruins show what life was like long ago. Some Maya work at these ruins. They tell stories about the past. Other Maya make a living selling goods. They sell rugs, blankets, and jewelry. Life has changed for the Maya. But much remains the same.

....

tourist – a visitor to a place

Stop and Think!

What is life like for the Maya today?

▼ **This Maya man is visiting a ruin to learn about the past.**

23

Recap

Describe how the Maya today are like the Maya of long ago.

Set Purpose

Learn more about the life of the ancient Maya.

CONNECT WHAT YOU HAVE LEARNED

The Maya
In the Past and Present

The ancient Maya were among the first people to live in the Americas. They had a rich culture. They built large cities. They made beautiful jewelry and art.

Here are some ideas that you learned about the ancient Maya.

- The ancient Maya lived in parts of Mexico and Central America.
- The ancient Maya were farmers.
- The ancient Maya lived in city-states ruled by chiefs.
- Today, many Maya follow the traditions of their ancestors.

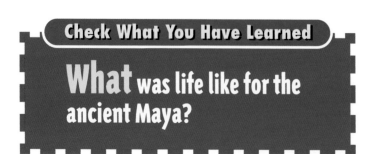

Check What You Have Learned

What was life like for the ancient Maya?

▲ Maya ruins are found in Mexico and Central America.

▲ Maize was an important crop for the ancient Maya.

▲ City-states were often built around pyramids.

▲ Weaving has been a part of Maya life since ancient times.

An Ancient Ball Game

▲ This hoop was used in the Maya ball game.

The Maya did not play baseball or soccer. They played a game using a rubber ball. Every city had a special ball court. People came to watch the game and cheer.

Two teams played the game. Players hit the ball with their shoulders, hips, or knees. They tried to bounce the ball through a hoop at one end of the court. The first team to score won the game.

▼ This modern drawing shows men playing the ancient Maya game.

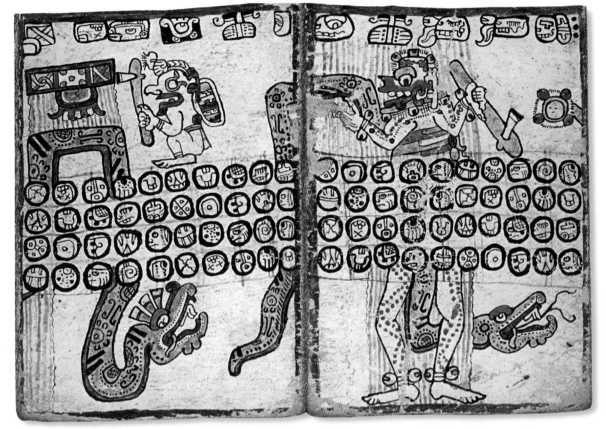

▲ This book is an ancient record of important dates.

Calendar Makers

The Maya created an early calendar. Their year was almost the same as our 365-day year. The Maya used their calendar to decide when to hold ceremonies. They also used it to decide when to plant crops. Today, some Maya still use the ancient calendar to choose wedding dates.

Ancient Stargazers

Almost everyone has looked at the stars. The Maya were stargazers, too. They built a special building to look at the stars and planets. That building is called an observatory.

The Maya were good astronomers. They saw the many stars that make up the Milky Way. They called the Milky Way the "World Tree."

The Maya could also predict when a solar eclipse would happen. A solar eclipse is when the moon hides part or all of the sun.

▼ These are ruins of the Maya observatory.

◀ This is the hieroglyph for "grass."

Picture Words

The Maya created the first system of writing in the Americas. They did not write with words, though. They wrote with hieroglyphs. Hieroglyphs are pictures and symbols.

The Maya used about 800 different hieroglyphs! Each one stood for a word, sound, or number. The writers told about wars, rulers, and celebrations.

Many kinds of words are used in this book. Here you will learn about words that have a suffix. You will also learn about words that are opposites.

Suffixes

A suffix is a group of letters added to the end of a word. A suffix changes the meaning of the word. Can you figure out what these new words mean?

power + ful = powerful

Ancient Maya chiefs were **powerful.** They had lots of power.

color + ful = colorful

Maya headdresses were **colorful.** They had lots of color.

Antonyms

An antonym is a word that means the opposite of another word. Look at the pairs of words below. What other antonyms do you know?

The ancient Maya built **big** pyramids.

They also built **small** homes that had just one room.

Weather in Central America is **warm.**

The Maya dress in light cotton clothes to keep **cool.**

Most people wore **plain** clothing.

Chiefs had **fancy** clothes.

Research and Write

Write About the Ancient Maya

You read about the Maya long ago. Now learn more about how they lived and worked. Why are the ancient Maya famous? Why do people study the Maya today?

Research

Collect books and reference materials, or go online.

Read and Take Notes

As you read, take notes and draw pictures.

Write

Write a paragraph telling two facts that you learned about the ancient Maya. Why are these facts interesting? What do they say about the Maya of long ago?

Read More About the Ancient Past

Find and read other books about ancient civilizations.
As you read, think about these questions.

- Why is this ancient civilization famous?
- How is this civilization like others in the past?
- What remains today from these ancient ways of life?

Books to Read

▲ Read more about the Maya people in the past and present.

▲ Learn how ancient Inca culture is preserved in modern-day Peru.

▲ Discover amazing facts about some of the earliest cultures in the world.

Glossary

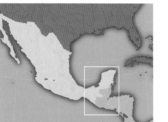

ancient (page 4)
Very old or from very long ago
Mexico and Central America have been home to the Maya since ancient times.

ceremony (page 9)
A formal act done on a special occasion
People sometimes went to pyramids for religious ceremonies.

chief (page 8)
The leader of a tribe of people
Each Maya city-state had a ruler, or chief.

city-state (page 8)
A settlement or city with its own government
Maya cities were called city-states.

jade (page 12)
A green stone
The ancient Maya made jewelry and statues from jade.

maize (page 11)
Corn
The most important crop was maize.

merchant (page 14)
A person who sells things
Some modern Maya are merchants, just as in ancient times.

pyramid (page 6)
A building with four sides that come together to form a point
The ancient Maya are famous for building pyramids.

ruins (page 6)
The remains of old buildings
Today, people still visit Maya ruins from ancient times.

tourist (page 23)
A visitor to a place
Tourists visit ancient Maya ruins to learn about the past.

valuable (page 13)
Worth a lot
The Maya traded valuable things, such as shells.

Index